Legacy

Kieran Davis

Legacy

Kieran Davis
Edited by Black Pear Press

First published in July 2018 by Black Pear Press
www.blackpear.net

ISBN 978-1-910322-73-4

Cover Photograph and Design Damien Davis
http://damiendavis.co.uk

Black Pear Press

Introduction

"He placed his ghost in the stone." (*Mythago Wood*, 2009, Robert Holdstock)

That sentence leapt off the page when reading this brave little fantasy; a bold statement delivering permanence. I loved the idea of being able to metaphysically indulge in one's legacy, forcibly push one's spirit into something like stone; a monolithic testament that should last several lifetimes.

I am desperate to leave a legacy, put as many thoughts on paper as possible. I relate to an interview between Maxine Kumin (Pulitzer Prize-winning poet) and Martha George Meek, where Kumin talks of the feeling that it seems necessary to leave a legacy of human thought and philosophy to prove we were sentient, intelligent beings—though prove to whom or what, I have no idea.

I only know I share that feeling of necessity and the ticking clock in my head is louder when I do not have a pen or pencil in my hand. Maxine said: "Always this sense the writer has, a kind of messianic thing: who will tell it if I do not? This is your assignment: to record it, to get it down, to save it for immortality."

This is another thought I have empathy with, worrying constantly if someone will record the thoughts, that maybe I should pen them just in case and now I am worrying about wasting time commenting on the thoughts of others rather than just recording my own.

It gets complicated because I wonder if someone will ever read this and think about my thoughts, thinking about another thinker. With me now thinking about them thinking about me thinking about what others are thinking my mind turns to jelly.

The interview mentioned appears in *To Make A Prairie* (Kumin, 1979) and goes on to discuss dreams (nightmares in particular) and how one who is strong willed and well-read can discern when they are dreaming but realise they must dream the dream through to its ultimate conclusion regardless of any concern or fear (safe in the knowledge that it is a dream and no physical damage should befall, though mental / psychological scars are likely and necessary for growth and learning).

I had an uncanny feeling when reading, having encountered this experience many times. My note books are littered with records of dreams and nightmares and much of my fantasy writing and mythology are born therein.

I have a recurring nightmare that has a very 'Tripods'-esque (relating to the excellent series of YA novels by John Christopher) feel to it, post-apocalyptic in a barren place clearly the product of disaster or much neglect. Above a bridge of colossal proportions, narrow and with a potent feeling of necessity even though it appears that it does not span anything but could possibly be a dried-up riverbed below.

I see crumbly, dusty soil and foliage, greenery giving way to browns and yellows but not autumnal as the sun is huge in the sky and hot, a blue and light purple sky with many a great avian soaring high. They are not birds I know in this world but certainly not dragons, griffins or similar from the worlds I usually dream of; the 'birds' look like single pencil strokes in a picture.

The bridge is high. I have vertigo, am sick and vulnerable. I am scared because, even if the fall does not kill me, the blade will if I land beneath the bridge because the span turns out to be an unbelievable guillotine with a lightning quick razor that descends as fast as a blink and then disappears faster.

I am facing an opponent, a terrifying man, a nemesis that has plagued me my whole life and is hell bent on destroying me. I am sick, scared, and sad. I am crying and, on occasion, I feel these things whilst thinking about the dream (when I am awake remembering) as it's awfully real.

It is a dream, I know it is a dream, I know what will happen, I know what must happen but still have to dream it through to the awful conclusion. I don't know when or how we start fighting but we do and it lasts forever (both experts in hand-to-hand combat and knowing each other's moves as if we were each other) and over in an instant simultaneously.

We each come close to falling several times, the terror of losing one's balance and grip (on reality as much as purchase on anything to retain an equilibrium). It is over. I do not recall the last blow, do not even see my foe fall but I know he has and then, impossibly—I am by his side though I did not jump, fall or climb down from the incredible height.

And the guillotine activates, I cringe as the head rolls away to reveal the face to me for the first time, a bit like Luke in Darth Vader's form when he goes in to the swamp of Dagobar during his Jedi training with Yoda (may all the deities bless George Lucas and may the force be with him always…I know I am a geek).

I see the face and it is horrible, terrifying, and hideous. The most awful, disgusting face ever, the scariest thing I have ever encountered. And I am exhausted, ashamed and aware that I must face him again and again and feel these awful things over and over though I have killed him (and not for the first time).

The face was mine, but I guess you saw that coming. I wonder at the dream sometimes and think I know why it is recurrent, the constant need to fight myself, the eternal internal struggle, the obvious truth that I am my own worst enemy and that I can be self-destructive (and intentionally on occasion, the complex and angry/compulsive fool that I can be).

I know this, have learned this, and have made efforts to change—years of sobriety, giving up smoking and dangerous life-style choices, making an effort to be nice, charitable and conscious of making a happy life for my children.

But the dream returns again and again and always as terrifying as the last time. I wonder if I will ever win outright and have to stop fighting with myself.

And so, dreams and digression aside—my legacy: I hope beyond hope, even pray sometimes (though to whom, I have no idea) that I am able to leave something clever or amusing that I will be remembered for, that will mark our race as sentient and intelligent beings; I long to place my ghost in the stone.

Kieran Davis

Publications

Lacuna (2016) Black Pear Press

Leg-a-cy (légga-si) n., *pl.*-**cies**. 1. Money or property bequeathed to someone by will. 2. Something handed down from an ancestor or predecessor, or from the past: *a legacy of madness.*

Dedication

For Jonathan, Oscar, Willow and Daisie, my true legacy. Never has a man been more proud to leave something so magical to the world.

Contents

When We Were Almost Young

Do you recall our tree, the blanket, a bed of hay?
The special feeling we called love, while others thought it play.
Do you remember railway track walks, always hand in hand?
Our elders thought us silly, they could never understand
how we felt that summer, when we lived at the lake,
an amazing season, yet I made one mistake,
and that was to let you go. Oh! How my heart was stung!
It's strange that we felt so much,
when we were almost young.

Now, years and miles between us, I still think of you,
wondering where and how you are, do you think of me too?
Do you recall the poetry, the time we spent in bed
just listening to music? One look, one touch…all said.
The days went on forever, the nights gone in a blink,
I remember you smiling always (that mischievous little wink),
do you remember laughter, how we had so much fun?
I miss your company and your kisses
from when we were almost young.

Haunts

Old houses, abandoned playgrounds,
that live on in my memory,
derelict dreams, your smile—
forever haunting me.
The ghosts of kisses echo
in my sensibility,
forgetting the phantoms,
an impossibility.
Favourite places leave traces,
faces, barely recalled,
but able to enchant
and keep me enthralled,
the dens where we played
'let's pretend'
and you stole your first
kiss from me;
where you went and how you died,
still a mystery.

The Audience Awaits

The audience shuffles in their seats,
the stage looms before the reader,
the night hides behind the curtain
and the poet waits to feed her,
whispering into the microphone,
to set an atmosphere,
words wander away, panic!
The pages disappear…

…as the audience awaits.

The world spins beneath him,
he stands on the precipice,
ghosts of failures find him,
as he sinks into the abyss,
the unquiet savage of sorrow,
doubt has found new premises,
courage flees the auditorium,
confidence, his nemesis…

…as the audience anticipates.

Scared to death, he takes a breath,
and opens up his eyes,
anything is possible
remembering, he tries.
Art and oratory venture forth,
surprising and delighting,
the poet performs, forgetting
the fright that he was fighting…

…the audience appreciates.

Those Brown Eyes

Those brown eyes,
the melting chocolate
that whispers of warmth,
a seduction of secrecy
and suggestion of stealth,
a guarded glance,
that relinquishes
the romance of the moment,
an atonement?
The portcullis of lashes
crashes down in a blink,
the wink I almost missed
as I kissed
those brown eyes.

Doubtlessly Busy

Busy mind thinking,
thinking about drinking,
drinking, lout, sinking,
sinking and winking,
out,
busy mind thinking,
doubt.

I Used To Bring You Flowers

I used to bring you flowers,
worship you with words,
sing to you as you slept,
but you never thanked me,
your expression frozen,
I wept and wept and wept,
and you would not comfort me,
ignored my tears, I feared
I could no longer be brave,
I wonder if you knew it was not
the cold that made me shudder,
but the silence of your grave.

Unstoppable

She looked as though
she were trying to see
right through the world
at something she needed
on the other side,
an impossible distance,
implausible, perhaps,
but that look,
that sheer determination,
dissipated any doubt
that she would achieve—
for she believed.
She was unstoppable.

Annoyed

Weightless ghosts, the hosts
of the bard's vanguard,
his army's armoury, harm for me
in my marred, die-hard disregard
for hypocrites like me.

Willow's Song

Apple pie lullaby,
just for you,
how I want to beautify
the world for you,
but a dragonfly lullaby,
will not do,
so my butterfly lullaby,
I sing for you.

Cherry pie lullaby,
just for you,
how I want to purify
the world for you,
but a dragonfly lullaby,
will not do,
so my butterfly lullaby,
I sing for you.

Cease

Some call it death
but I like to think,
we did not wake,
stayed on the brink
of reality's precipice,
unconscious or dreaming,
when no one can hear you,
there's no point in screaming.

Duly Noted!

All these notes, untouched,
the thoughts and ideas
left idle,
dormant on scraps
of peppered parchment, salted
with salient silence;
the condiments of commonplace
books. My miscellany.

Event Horizon

Eyes, like aspergillums,
an intermittent trickle
and sprinkle of salt waters,
that sing hymns and belt out
anthems, simultaneously.
Famously, the fickle fates
of fathers, are the sires
to daughters of destiny,
kings that felt doubt.
Posthumously,
the poet's page reaches out,
a crime, defying time,
most humorously.

Bridge Of Time

I reach the woods, marvelling at the magnificence
of the butterflies, as they dance like faeries around
me, it's been too long since I have been back here.
I walk to the site of the broken bridge, (now a high,
sturdy platform spanning the river) and recall, the
summers here, building makeshift bridges with friends,
hoping that we'd run the whole of the woods. Travellers
would often come to watch our labours with amusement,
they were grateful for its completion. Fewer and fewer
of us would return to build our bridge (that the river
would claim each winter) and one summer, I alone came
to make that crossing. The waters had risen to claim my
valiant efforts when I returned. I smile, watching the
river rush by on its endless journey, and I return to the
woodland path, my feet knowing, every step of a trail
my memory had almost forgotten.

Mercy

(For My Biscuits)

The music of chance,
the lottery of life's flavour,
the destiny of the dance,
survives, beloved saviour,
the magic of our marriage,
the majesty in your eyes,
phoenix of my fate,
the love that never dies.

Son Shine

I tried to teach you lessons
that I never learned,
preached about passions,
the bridges I burned,
and I spoke of the world
like it was somewhere I had been,
warned you away from girls,
take it all away, unclean,
that anthem, that *screamer*,
I almost coughed up a lung,
this daft, old daydreamer,
born old to die young,
thankfully, you did not listen,
too much like your dad,
I leave proud tears to glisten
on the memories we've had.

Overpriced Territory

The path, worn and wound
round by the wounded
who followed the poor
souls, now swallowed
and burned. So few returned.

Sceptic

Is it this wicked world,
that makes a sceptic,
or a wicked heart?

Roam

Restless gypsy,
my soul seeks
streets, unknown,
a relative reality,
I have no wish to roam,
I try not to let my mind
wander far,
for it does not know its way home.

Undressed

There needs to be an urgency,
an emergency of feeling
for poetry to reach out
and leave the reader reeling.
The poem is a potion
of emotion for the poet,
who imbibes life like tequila,
but through whiskey wisdom,
shows it.

Wish

Brume be gone,
I seek the sun,
though it be
a winter one
that is replete
of heat, still I
search for saviours
in the sky.

A Pensive Child

Watching out the window,
staring into space,
such a pensive child,
that look upon his face,
far away, but no fantasy,
not the ache of wanderlust,
I think I witnessed the spark,
the genesis of genius,
a busy mind, thinking,
instead of having fun,
no interest in toys,
not *this* little one,
he wants to read *all* the books,
he *needs* to write a story,
already inviting other worlds
to know the boy before me.
Games remain unplayed,
not bothered with treats, well earned,
too lost in absorbing,
the lessons in life,
yet to be learned.

Awe

When I am a relic,
my life become yore,
young gods will wake
and whisper of war.

When I am a memory
you cease to explore,
your gods will take
their leave like before.

When I am a legend,
grief's guarantor,
the gods you forsake
will forgive the flaw.

When I am a myth,
dismissed and no more,
old gods will break
like waves on the shore.

Banish, Not Vanish

He sits up in bed,
his hair matted with sweat
pouring down his body,
he rubs his eyes.
Just a dream, that's all,
and he lies back,
eyes wide, searching the darkness.
Becoming accustomed to the lack of light,
he sees vague outlines,
objects, visions, passing before his eyes.
Shouts.
Screams:
"John, NO! "
The car.
The boy.
His face.
Running,
call an ambulance,
tell his family.
Run?
Is that all you could do?
and his eyes close,
and he drifts back to sleep,
and the dream.

Bravado

When versus the verses,
uncreative cabal curses.
Rhymer rehearses.

Fleeting

Beauty, but an illusion,
a powerful poison,
meticulous confusion.

Pang

The progeny of the poet
play perfect parts
in piecing the puzzle
together. Clever.

Dedicated

(Or 'Thank You')

Thank you.
For keeping my secrets,
and telling my lies,
for saving my soul
and drying my eyes,
for holding my hand
and kissing my head,
for breathing new life
into dreams I thought dead,
for giving and living,
forgiving me,
thank you, thank you
for loving me.

Dreamy Woodland

The whispering woods,
the talk of the trees,
the lies on the leaves
and the beautiful breeze,
a susurrus of secrets,
a smell of sweetness,
a perfect paradigm
of pictorial completeness.

Denial

That's not him, lying there, that's not him,
that's not him, dying there, that's not him,
that's someone else that looks like him,
the ghost of a man, visage, grim, that's not him.
Most of the man, now a memory,
this ghost of a man, so far from me,
that's not him, lying there, that's not him.
That's not him, so sorry,
that's not him, it can't be!
That's not him, that's not him.

Happy Sausages

'Happy sausages' is a silly sound
and I like it very much,
my youngest son made me say it,
for photo fun and such,
I could not help but smile and laugh,
titter at temptation,
to embrace a happiness thought lost,
through worry and frustration.
So, thank you, Oscar, beloved boy,
for the interruption.
I entertain a smile as I say:
'Happy sausages' again!

Paranoia

(Or 'Panic')

Distrustful, mistrustful,
completely insecure,
fearful and suspicious,
paranoia's overture,
a glance over my shoulder,
I swear someone said my name,
a paramour pickled my past,
I was burnt by an old flame
whose memory tickles,
and trickles lazily,
in to a river of reverie,
in which I splash crazily,
until I cannot tread water,
the flood of feeling is oceanic,
I start to drown as I go down,
distressed and in a panic.

Unsubtle City

Labyrinthine lanes,
tangled web of walled-in walks,
the bustle of hustlers
and hobos who muster
the courage to traverse,
the adverse avenues
that the muse
of a city-slicker, stalks.

The Hanging Tree

Dark dendriform,
oh, how I fear,
mad monument,
of yesteryear,
your boughs engraved,
with scratch of rope,
where damned, condemned,
lost faith, all hope,
and danced their last,
as life fled thee,
dark dendriform,
the hanging tree.

Sword

(An Acrostic)

Surviving,
when
others,
readily
die.

Spooked

I wake up screaming, but no one hears me,
I hold the covers tight over my head,
on the count of three,
I tear out of my bedroom faster
than the Millennium Falcon, and down the stairs,
but my parents tell me I am being silly.
I am so afraid of the nightmares,
I won't go back to bed and I tell them:
   "No."
Rookie mistake to make,
I am made to stand facing the wall,
until I am 'ready' to go back to bed,
whilst they watch Hammer horror movies
on the television,
I stand for what seems like hours,
glaring at the boring wallpaper,
not bothering to count the flowers thereon,
as I know there are three hundred and seventy-seven.
I have counted them so many times
I would never need another recount.
And so eventually, I climb the stairs, unmissed.
Entering the room, fearful
of what is behind the door
or in my cupboard,
I dive back into bed and pull up the covers,
squeezing my eyes tight in terror,
I just know that they are out there waiting,
biding their time until I peek,
and then they will get me…
MONSTERS!

Leave A Legacy

(Or 'I Insist')

Tear down the Titans,
grapple with the gods,
wage war with words,
that will beat the odds,
will the quill,
to chew what was bitten,
with powerful penmanship,
history is written.

Porcelain

I know you're not shatterproof,
though not a china doll,
your façade, prettily painted.
My faint heart aches to see
beyond the spoof,
inside, the soul breaks,
a tainted tattoo.

Camera-shy

Just out of shot,
the funny face
that they were all smiling at, not forgotten,
though not in the picture,
the name,
etched forever
on the edge of the frame,
in all of our hearts,
the game bird,
that one word,
which elicits smiles still:
Nana.

Carry

The whispers of the free, the free,
carry you to the sea, the sea,
marry your heart to me, to me,
tarry not in misery.

The whispers of the free, the free,
carry you to the sea, the sea,
marry your heart to me, to me,
carry a kiss for me.

Carry a kiss for me,
marry your heart to me.

Blanket

Where does the winter go?
I never dare to ask,
the weather, ever clever,
wears a wicked mask.

The Quickening

Brave new worlds
will wonder
at the thunder
in the skies,
my voice, your kiss,
your curse, your choice,
I live on in your lies.

Writer

Sometimes, I would sit
with a fresh piece of paper
and a pencil that I would
will the life into, just
empty myself onto the page
until words became
sentences and, subsequently,
something of meaning,
possibly...
of some worth.
Whether I penned a poem
or scribbled an appendix
for my mythology
(or simply sated my need
to see thoughts collected,
in the way only a writer can),
I would breathe more easily;
knowing I had accomplished
something in my day.
Strange, how only my peers
appreciate such nonsense,
and recognize my reality,
my version of the truth;
pertaining to the nature
of such things.
Similar souls ache to be
amused by the muse
and refuse to be abused.

United

A brave breeze, fanned
by angels' wings,
when yesterday wore
the mask of tomorrow,
and fervid extremists
failed humanity, achieving
A greater unity than that
which they tried to disrupt.
Hungry for retaliation,
a desperate urge to purge
this world of those we judge
too easily,
and we would serve them
their undeserved desire
on that clichéd silver platter.
How does a hate-filled heart forgive!
We will not be bowed,
we will not be bullied,
we will be brothers and sisters.
We will love, be loving, and be loved.

Think!

If only these words
would write themselves,
then I could think,
without concern
for trivia,
or losing focus,
losing imaginings,
the melodramatic tragedy
of a misplaced notebook,
or a pen, run out of ink.
Think!

Tiny Little Pub Poem

(For The Old Wolf & Sahm King)

Laugh, laugh!
Laugh loud and clear!
Dance on the tables
and drink all the beer!

The Ghost Of A Kiss

I feel the ghost of a kiss on my neck,
like a breath, mistakenly shared,
whored away and forgotten, shelved,
with God for safe-keeping, spared
the need for dusting because I am in
the display cabinet with the best china,
only to be used at Christmas,
(the kiss, passed to a hungry diner)
and the ghost, holy or otherwise,
shuns the posh plates and their symbolism,
curious with the memory of the kiss,
and the consequence of emotional vandalism,
whilst God (who crept in when I was not looking)
begins his Punch 'n' Judy show
in my soul, the ghost of a kiss reminding me,
someone must have left open a window.

The Djinn Done-in

A wish for patience, wasted,
if one cannot afford
the longevity required to reap
the desired reward.

Phantoms

Ethereal images, imaginings perhaps,
surreal ideals, immaterial and fading,
the dream-like ghosts that haunt those
waking moments, when the mind,
barely aware, and still scared of the night,
stumbles and fumbles for a fragment
of fantasy, with which to cling to
in the grim reality, the banality
of the tempting attempt to avoid
inevitable eventuality. Eventuality.

Poem To Willow

I love that you're inquisitive,
and like to try things, new,
the things that don't go in your mouth,
are now so very few,
and though you are all gums
and have no teeth with which to chew,
please, please! Stop eating pages,
MY books are not for you!

Practice

Meticulous scrivener,
sat, statuesque,
careful calligrapher
at his desk,
consists of
poetry, painted,
resists love,
notary, acquainted.

Not Conservative

Memory is susceptible to flaw,
hence we chronicle in notebooks,
engrave glyphs and depict
our perceived history
as if it happens to someone else.
We delve into dictionaries
and inflict fiction, unstable fable,
nonsense news, abused
and juxtaposed by journalists,
exposed to endeavours we fear
to fathom, the dictum of dictators
that *we* voted into office,
and called names like the variant
of an orifice.
We push pens over paper,
A collective caper of friction
and fallacy, believed. Deceived.
Received, democracy diluted,
politics—polluted.

Mulch

'Mulch' is a great word,
though not particularly pretty,
it is oozing and disgusting,
and, let's face it, somewhat shitty,
but it's perfect immolation,
the forest's poison of choice,
feeds and breeds, and then succeeds,
disembodied, voice.

Amazing

(For Alan Durham)

Fatherly love, how else can I describe?
For what you gave me, I could just imbibe,
whenever I saw the warmth of your smile,
I knew that life was all worthwhile.

Bridge, Absurd

At a time when illogicality
is tempered with the truth,
devised by mythmakers
who ascend a bridge of birds
to behold love
in its most divine and raw form,
normality is the device
of Da Vinci, Icarus' spirit
reborn, forlorn sceptics
breathe belief, a true god,
forged in the womb
of sex mad scientists gone
insane…again.

Don't Speak

(Or 'Grief')

There are not the words
to assuage your grief,
there never are, nor will there be.
Pain beyond belief,
you want constant company.
But as your departed,
emptied you of all but loss,
and silence deafens,
and sound offends,
just breathing is breaking
your heart with vehemence.

Cradle Of Cruelty

Every detail of the final moment,
written on the corpse's face,
recorded for my duration,
in the terror of my memories.

Children

Children, children, children,
one of my favourite words,
the chitter-chatter sound
reminds me of busy birds.
Children, children, children,
I love the art of their laughter,
the lilting, tickling giggle
that echoes ever after.

Impartial Skies

I am the spirit of winter,
always present in your absence,
a page in someone else's history book,
I stare into the water
until I see *beyond* the reflection,
a quiet introvert with a loud soul,
my disgusting loveliness
a dark sun dying
in impartial skies.

Inconceivable

Take the poet to the hospice,
when the playwright leaves the jail,
the vinegar of ingratitude
becomes afflicted with language.
A note, not worth noticing, is noted,
and exchanged for a glass of pity,
and the criminals are like a cancer.
They spread rumours of tumours,
and myriad myths of malaise,
for their own amusement, the abuse,
obtuse and overlooked, the cacophony
of their chaos; erased in minds
that have long rejected euphoria.
That legend, no longer believed achievable,
that story, that poem, inconceivable.

Love

Love sees through the rain,
to discover cerulean skies,
love sees you mirrored
in each other's eyes.
Love is literature,
poetry in motion,
love lives on your lips,
and leaves only devotion.
Love, like a magic spell,
a perfect, peculiar pleasure,
love says 'I cherish you',
your heart, something I treasure.

Note To Self

Wipe the page,
prepare the stage,
you know the world is waiting!
Don't make an excuse,
you must, just refuse
to keep procrastinating.
Don't be absurd,
write down a word,
type if you have no quill,
a crayon is fine,
a pencil, sublime,
write with whatever you will,
plot, poem, caper,
put it on paper!
A napkin, a loo roll will do!
Because you know if you don't,
the world simply won't,
care that you're just cross with you!

Scared Of Seaside Shadows

I gaze at gulls that glide
halfway from heaven,
tide, ebbing and webbing, disturbed,
perturbed by things that scuttle
on rocks, shocks, unsubtle.
I swiftly leave my seat,
my discomfort, complete.

The Damned, Unmanned

It is amazing
what a coward
can accomplish,
desperate measures
are taken,
the truth we embellish,
the lies
we have forsaken,
taken for granted,
supplanted.
The slavery of bravery
be damned,
for the brand
of a coward's conniving
is to be surviving
all, even unmanned.

Youth Is Wasted On The Young

A smile meets my imperfections,
an acknowledgement of a burning son,
the heart racing when tracing youth
that is wasted on the young.

A smile like an affectation,
an awful judgement, poor pun,
that parts the lacing, facing youth
that is wasted on the young.

A smile, but a deflection
and false encouragement, undone,
then embracing a shell, encasing youth
that is wasted on the young.

A smile, like an erroneous attraction,
an instrument of the perfect sun,
the fool chasing and wasting youth
that is wasted on the young.

A smile, that subtle distraction,
as fulfilment fakes a hit-and-run,
this defacing and replacing youth
that is wasted on the young.

Zephyr

Momentarily insubstantial,
lonely revenant, circumstantial,
the heart of the hurricane, detrimental,
a heretic deemed elemental,
inebriated on the wine of wind
pixilated, god just grinned.

Give Up?

Am I so chimerical
that reality has receded?
My soul-sworn oath
has both ensured a victory of vision
and immured my chance
of eradicating the division,
multiple personality—conceded.

Epitaph, Entreated

It's just my bones that lie here,
I want it written on my grave,
as my soul was sold so long ago,
so keep your prayers, and save
your tears; for the years I gave you
are worth more than the loss.
Wherever I am, I love you,
don't be cross.
I ask one last thing,
my one wish, my final boon,
live your life, be free and please;
don't come and see me soon.

Fallacy

Dance of destruction,
a day of dissonance,
the zounds of sounds,
unquiet confounds
creative circumstance,
slim chance of enchanting,
implanting doubt,
the shock of writers' block,
a crock of shit, thrown out.

Moments

(Or 'Hold Still' Or 'Photographs Of Dead Friends')

(i)
Photographs of dead friends,
images of happiness,
perceived perfection,
captured in those
'smile for the camera' moments
that could last a lifetime,
even though their flickering
existences have ceased;
blown out like candles
in the hands of evil iconoclasts
who would melt those memories.

(ii)
"Say cheese!"
Please.
I beg the picture,
willing the departed
to hear a prayer
I am certain God did not.
Still within those
well documented stages,
despite the years
and miles between me
and their graves.
Not at all sure that I grieve,
as I still do not believe,
and I am still angry,
and I still cry,
because they die—
every time, every single time
I hold that still frame.

Their name, though whispered,
causes cataclysms.

(iii)
Photographs of dead friends,
past glories thought
never to be relived,
until someone catches me looking
at those cheeky grins;
and asks me who they are.
I hesitate, about to say
'who they *were*,'
but they *are*,
for they live on
in more than these glossy keepsakes,
when I tell their stories,
not anecdotes
to occasionally entertain,
but legends.

An Al-mighty Mate

(For Alan Durham)

A fatherly smile,
you nod, knowingly,
as the years leave my eyes,
understanding, suddenly,
that it is okay to enjoy
for enjoyment's sake,
I had forgotten, but will try not
to again make that mistake.

Tree Terror

If a tree were a sentient being,
I wonder if it would panic,
fearing every Autumn may be its last,
as it sheds its leaves, worrying
that it was falling apart
as winter approached and threatened
an eternal freeze, implying
that there would be no rebirth,
no renewal, that the natural sugars,
the soul required would be withheld.
Some of the trees look depressed,
mighty boughs, now bare, seem scared,
as if they know some terrible truth
that mankind could not cope
with the copious attacks of the elements,
have left the leafless looking weathered,
yet they remain stoic sentinels,
their shoulders still broad as if able
to carry the weight of worlds,
as yet unknown to us. A wonder,
that we, the trees' greatest enemy,
love them so much and fear for them,
hoping they know no such terror.
Would I stand so brave
in an encounter with blade or flame?
Why can I not be so strong
in the face of uncertainty and loss?
If only I could give as much to the world.

Weathered

The sky starts crying poetry,
a deluge, damaging a bard's
appearance before an audience.
Hail, biting like glass shards;
soaked and shirtless, sobbing,
the poet falls on bended knee;
shadows, wet and whispering,
the storm's sweet symphony.

Sorrow sails in paper boats,
from a jaded journal's pages,
on a new-born stream of broken dreams
the rain corrects the sage's
misinterpretation
of maltreatment and neglect.
The poet ponders the penalty
paid for the chance to reflect.

Bare

The cast iron coal bucket,
a memory of fires,
the cold, black metal,
so many dead desires,
the red brick hearth,
the panelled walls,
and winding stair,
the empty halls,
ash stirred, without a word,
the breeze breathes down the chimney,
my mantle bowed by a heavy load,
feeling, no longer in me.

Darling Daughter

Goodnight, baby girl,
my darling daughter,
my daughter!
How marvellous to say,
to hear out loud,
a son's sister
of whom I am so proud,
my heart lifts
and I smile, knowing joy
I had not believed possible,
happy in the quiet
of the night as I gaze
at my sleeping little lady.
Goodnight,
my precious, goodnight.
Oh, my darling daughter.

Perfect

(For Polly Stretton)

Ponderer of poems,
precious,
you reflect, I then see,
under no illusion,
you remain perfect to *me*.
Let me have my heroes,
they make me want to be,
more than the child
that so many people see.
Ponderer of poems,
precious,
I reflect, you see,
under no illusion,
you remain perfect to *me*.

Tunnels

Time has eroded
the terror once evoked
by tunnels, an error?
Faith provoked me
to find courage,
I discouraged
my son from worrying,
hurrying to misbehave,
I laughed so I looked brave.

Black

It is hard to keep up the charade,
the part I played in the parade,
no surprise, the glittering eyes
evict the smile as I fade.
My shirt, white and stark against the dark
of my tie, the choking garrotte,
being someone I'm not.
"I'm fine." I laugh and I joke,
"I'm just off out for a smoke."
But the truth is, on my own,
I feel less alone,
for the company makes me cross.
"So sorry for your loss,"
echoes on and on,
no comfort now you're gone.

Frog Snog

The stories we were told as children,
the fairy tales we suckled,
were lovely lies that could never
prepare us for the moment
when, as old men, we would realise,
we did not become princes
when kissed, but kings, sovereigns
of sorrow, in love
with the concept of possibility, but attracted
to doubt;
married to history.

Love Literature

I am impelled,
my addiction must be fed,
words must be written,
smitten, books must be read,
hungry for history,
I salivate and dribble,
no restriction for my fiction,
I suck up the scribble
and maul in my mind's maw,
the letters, every sentence,
some say a guilty pleasure
but I show no repentance.

00:56

I am your audience,
I hear your voice,
your beautiful soul
and poison of choice.
Read to me, plead to me,
beg me to know you,
one page of bravery,
just goes to show you
that poetry is possible
if you just believe,
make it happen;
you can achieve!

Destination

Evening comes
and I sit,
alone,
as usual it seems of late;
doing what I do best:
Thinking.

There are many paths,
a man can take,
and many paths of others
that a man will cross
in just one lifetime,
but there are times,
when all those paths,
seem to lead
to one destination,
and when that destination,
is despair,
something within the human soul,
dies.

Searching For Sanity

(For Tony Judge, Written Whilst Reading 'Sirocco Express')

There came a point in the story when I realised,
this was not entirely a work of fiction.
I touched the precious page, reaching into the book,
a compulsion to sniff the ink and be a part
of the person who bled for me to remember,
the character lay there in the desert, staring
up at the stars with the world spinning beneath him,
the way I used to by the lake or in the woods,
becoming one with a universe that had forsaken me,
or so I thought. That perfect moment, I would
stare out to sea, find the horizon I could no longer chase,
and discover the fracture in reality,
where one could not discern where the ocean stopped
and the sky began, that cataclysmic event,
when clarity exploded in my soul with violent silence.
I spent a lifetime trying to recapture that instant,
opening my throat to imbibe destiny but forgetting to
swallow,
fate escaping as I exhaled and choked down the urge—
to expire. I forget to regret, searching for sanity.

Seek Not The Moon

Bring me the last horizon,
sing me the lost sunset,
try to dry your eyes, son,
you're not dying yet,
bring me the last horizon,
sacrifice the night,
seek not the moon
you'll see too soon
the sky, yet shy of light,
bring the last horizon,
sing me the lost sunset,
try to dry your eyes, son,
you're not dying yet.

Rejuvenate To Judge

Constantly reanimated,
my resistance to existence,
diluted, polluted, attributed,
a clean sound,
a pain, profound,
I am examined
with persistence.

Reflect

An active volcano
chronicles
the arena of ancients
with distilled choices,
voices
heard by those who can
endure more
than you can ever inflict,
the fear that affects
like killer kuru,
the clouded mirror
of my guru reflects,
reflects
the catholicon of love.

What Is Love?

Was it not we, the poets,
that invented this cruel notion?
The false pretence of an emotion,
so wholly unattainable and yet,
in contradiction,
all consuming and smothering,
completely destroyed,
beautifully reborn,
the one thing that will rejuvenate,
and simultaneously be the end of us all.
What is love?
A word so easily pounced upon,
and offered up in hope,
to hook a companion,
to initiate sex,
to live, to lie, to give, to die,
we have made it too perfect,
no poor soul can ever meet,
the impossible criteria,
that governs what we have made the world believe
are the requirements.
Though love is not necessarily about wants,
needs or even desires,
but it is necessary,
it is trust, faith and quite simply says:
I cherish you.

Urn Earned

I looked into the urn, kissed
you goodbye and saw,
something previously missed,
that I could not ignore,
a tale told twice
with an alternative ending,
your ashes were a story,
with an epilogue, still pending.

Where Did The Audience Go?

I sometimes think I would like,
to be adored and yet…ignored,
have an audience that applaud,
and appreciate but remain,
quiet, looking elsewhere.

I sometimes think I should strike,
every word yet to be heard,
from the page, absurd!
This one must refrain,
restrain the urge to tear!

Grave Error

That hole in the ground,
is too small to house
someone that meant
so very much to me,
the stone that will mark
where we buried you,
will never say anything
worthy enough,
and the memories of your
existence, the lessons
we learned from you,
the laughter and the love.
All that has been stolen
from us, makes us want
to lie down, in that hole
in the ground, give in,
and give up. Just give up.

Greaser

(Or 'As Your Guitar Lies Sleeping')

I wondered what chords you strummed in your dreams,
as your guitar lay sleeping in your arms, unharmed
by the arguments in my head, I fed you the lies,
you wanted to hear, so you could feel safe,
your fingers twitch and I fear you will wake, break
the silence with your violent orchestra, your frustrations,
fuelled with the vast libations you practically inhaled,
the challenge of children and a 'normal life',
aging you before it could be realised, the shackles
were forged by a man wearing your face, sharing your shame,
whistling what you would only dare to whisper,
whilst you mastered the art of fakery,
raping your own dreams instead of dusting them off,
and the motorbike man who didn't give a damn, died,
as your guitar lay sleeping in your arms, unharmed.

Invaders

For a moment,
I almost felt naughty
for listening.
My pristine page,
taunting the chewed pencil
as I try to capture characters
through an exercise
suggested in a magazine.
But then I see
I am not alone
in my invasion of privacy,
that knowing smile
across the café,
I swear I saw a wink
that said:
'You made it into
my notebook too."

Mourning Song

The sound of my own heartbeat,
breaks the silence in my soul,
you leave me without a purpose,
an empty life without a goal,
your passing leaves me barren,
more a wasteland than a man,
my spirit is tempestuous
and longs to feel your hand.

Burn me or bury me,
but shed no tear,
you said unto me,
but, my love, I fear
I cannot keep that promise,
I must break my word,
for water comes unto my eyes
and my heart will be heard,
screaming for you in the night,
crying out your name,
I weep until I sleep tonight,
I cry for love, in vain,
you have been stolen from me,
long before your time,
I am left in such despair,
my soul now frost and rime.

Lonely and forgotten,
I linger in these lands,
realms of hate and shadow,
where no one understands,
what it is to have loved and lost,
someone as precious as you,
you were my day, my night, my faith,
my one, my one love, true.

Proof Professed

If I am to fear nothing,
must I then, love nothing?
I fear sleep but hold
no affection for it, I dislike
the loss of time immensely,
the control forced upon
my physicality, perhaps
it is this prison of flesh,
the very body I reside in
that I fear, for its weakness
and lack of reliability,
the linear confinement of meat.
If I am to fear nothing,
must I then prove nothing?
The page would be pointless,
records made redundant,
literature left as litter,
but the thinker, regardless
of whichever 'ology' they
profess to love or learn,
would counter,
never able to abate debate, as,
whether points need to be proven,
or not, thoughts will be thought,
and I *fear*, sleep will find me,
before the words are able to.

Reconciliation

Beckoning for a reckoning,
your soul calls out to mine,
one reflects, mutual neglect,
is it time now, brother, mine?

Red Pen

Bleeding ink, I like to think,
the poet, so hard, tries,
better dead than left unread,
agonizing demise,
the page, unturned, best books be burned,
defies the lies and lessons, learned,
bleeding ink, I like to think,
and drink to deaths, unearned,
bleeding ink, I like to think,
replace the case, adjourned.

Melody

The sound of children laughing,
joy to watch them play,
the sound of children laughing,
the innocent display.
The sound of children laughing,
fills the heart with such cheer,
the sound of children laughing,
songs only souls can hear.

Sentient Thought

Language, a libation,
the salvation of the damned,
the drink of thinkers,
no nation understands.
I was born before creation,
the coming of man,
preceding believers,
God, I am.
Wordsmiths worship me,
the painting in the cave,
I am unable in the cradle—
but I will mark your grave...

The Music Of Life

The laughter of my children,
the smile from my wife,
the most majestic melody,
that is the music of life!

Served

I went to the pub
and I wrote a poem,
blocking out the cacophony,
the carefree, casual
drinkers, thinking
of thinkers as I sipped
and slipped onto a page,
my stage. This social hub,
stocking every writer's trophy,
the cider-soaked sage.

I Can't Hear You

I live on in the world
that you left behind,
your smorgasbord morgue,
waiting for the hunger
of my younger self.
"See you in hell," you said,
but you must have gone
somewhere else instead.

Rusty Sword

This is not your swaying,
in time's winds of change, lamented,
this is what your delaying
meant, to be sadly pretended.

This is not your fraying,
not that which may be mended,
this is what your slaying
meant, to be abruptly ended.

This is not your waylaying
of emotions, regimented,
this is what your displaying
meant, to be so malcontented.

This is not your fraying,
not that which can be mended,
this is what your slaying,
meant, to be abruptly ended.

This is not your paying
of debts once represented,
this is what your betraying
meant, to be our fate, cemented.

This is not your fraying,
not that which may be mended,
this is what your slaying,
meant, to be abruptly ended.

This is not your praying,
for tomorrows, yet demented,
this is what your staying
meant, to be for hope prevented.

Oscar Pickle Pants

The nickname makes me smile,
and then I sigh, content,
pleased to be a parent,
happy to be a husband,
delighted to be a daddy,
my boys make me so proud,
their happiness fills me with joy,
and Oscar, our newest arrival,
is so handsome like his brother,
such a wicked little smile!
I laugh, knowing the smell
is another nappy full of 'pickle!'

Complete

Daisie dreaming,
Daddy, dear,
enchanting, easy
to endear,
little wonder,
tiny treat,
family,
now complete.

Paranoid?

I **am** getting paranoid,
seeing ghosts that are not there,
angels look at me in the *loud silence*,
their forlorn gazes,
grating my soul with their sad expressions,
their lack of iteration,
wearing heavy on my heart.

Invasion

Memories of long ago,
a startling discovery,
fate failed to forge the faithful,
and said farewell to recovery,
mercy, the miracle,
that might mend mankind,
but blame divides, shame overrides,
are we, by dictators, defined?

Shelly's Slave

Stitched together
from odds and sods,
the gift of graves
and grief of gods,
they call *me* 'monster',
Frankenstein,
I'll murder the master
and make me mine.

The Mother Of All Addicts

Forced to forget,
regret reborn,
the failure of faith,
reality, torn,
the veil,
her reminder
of love that still
binds her
to a son she swore
forever lost,
sadness, madness,
such a cost.

Tears For Tana

Winter finds the broken-hearted,
malcontented, disenchanted,
disappointed, our departed
left for shores, as yet, uncharted,
love has grown and flown, alone,
an abyssal maw, an undertone,
once more, cancer has outsmarted
but cannot kill what you imparted,
for your wisdom, warmth and life still give,
and in our hearts, will ever live.

Justify The Lie

Silver shining,
gliding,
like starlight
seeking shade,
I fade.
Mining the memory,
climbing urgently,
ironing out the creases
in the thesis,
the justification
for emancipation,
we discuss the injustice.

The Page

I stare blankly at the page,
the stark white, empty space,
teasing me,
daring me to do something,
anything to fill the void.
The page taunts me,
whispering like a pretend best friend,
beautiful lies and ugly truths,
testing me, the 'writer'
and doubting my ability
to control the page's insatiable hunger
for poetry or prose (any words, I suppose).
I sit quietly and reflect,
wondering if inspiration will find me,
if I wait long enough.
Words wither if produced vehemently,
and fail to impress even myself
if delivered with unnecessary vocabulary,
but then I realise:
(whilst seething inwardly
at my recent lack of literary productivity)
that I am not alone in my thoughts,
as I stare blankly at the page.

Unbelievers

Do gods die the deaths
of mortals, deserving grief?
or do they merely slumber,
awaiting stray belief?
omnipotence turns
to impotence,
important prayers
a pretence,
a dangerous inkling,
catalyst of cataclysm,
the thunderstruck,
cluster-fuck of atheism.

Left Behind

These are the thoughts, those were the days,
before you cost me my innocence and went away,
there was laughter and wonder, a delicious daze,
of friendship and family that would forever stay,
in a madness of memories as we set ablaze,
the nights with enchantment, wherever we lay,
these are the thoughts, those were the days,
before you cost me my innocence and went away.

Kiss

The silence is not so terrifying now, the stillness
of the afternoon, almost soothing, the quiet
used to be found somewhat lacking but now my autumn
has no need for entertainment. I do not require
substance in the intermission, now that I have found
you. The peace that I have never known (before you)
lays anchor at a calm shore, the thunder gods
of heaven should bow down and acknowledge you,
because of the power in your kiss and it's delicious...

Majesty.

Live On

Some say I work too hard
to be remembered,
and I wonder what the catalyst
for this obsession is,
it creeps around the edge
of consciousness,
taunting any thread of sanity,
and scares the shit out of me,
so I plough on through the pages,
trying to survive the ages.

Slipping Into Sleep

Sweet certain outcome,
I have waited for your embrace,
brother mine, night divine,
how well I know your face,
to sit by your side in the great divide,
with the banishment of breath,
is to kiss the abyss and those I miss,
so welcome, little death.

Unconvinced

The mind shattered like a glass,
the revelation, evolving
into a dark genesis, a catalyst,
for chaos and the kindred
spirit of the child betrayed,
displayed as a grim trophy,
that reminded one of shame,
the name of hollow vengeance.

Wounded

The body heals, bones mend,
flesh regenerates in a fashion,
but the mind knows no scar tissue,
a fracture becomes a fissure
and, in time, a canyon; where careless
words whisper to the depths of
despair. Take care. Take care.

Manuscript

Familiar with the book,
I can not recall the title,
the author's name eludes me.
I am certain that the cover
has a different illustration
to the one I knew so well,
perhaps an earlier edition. I remember
the colours, the silver lettering
and the greens or blues
in the artwork, the cracked spine
announcing loudly that it is loved,
and the pages are easy to turn,
obviously thumbed often,
it must be a popular volume,
a consistently cherished codex.
I check my enchiridion to further
impress myself, and (to be honest)
show off, though all that likely
happens is a reader will bore easily
of unnecessary glossy vocabulary
and the tangent I have diverted
from the elusive title of that terrific
tome; that marvellous manuscript!

Nothing Is Trivial

Make the most of today,
of each moment,
revel in your existence,
ensuring these episodes
of excellence
do not become 'those good old days',
but a continuation
of celebration,
that well-spring of wonder,
a ripple in the river
of your happiness,
as you continue
to forget regret,
remembering,
nothing is trivial,
and anything
is possible.

Sad

It is strange how the fallen,
are able to move us to tears,
when the miles are as far
between us as the years,
their bodies not forgotten,
though long in the ground,
their ashes, now so distant,
on a breeze not to be found.

We Regret

We dislike all that we are not,
fear everything we are
and that which we do not understand
(especially anything different from
what we deem—urgh—'normal'),
we hate ourselves for aging
and/or becoming weak, stressed
of heart, or worse—of mind...
we find our vainglorious past,
pulling faces from a misperceived
image in the looking glass,
a poor projection, false reflection,
our tired eyes misconceive
a god-like imagining,
that flawless forgery
we are so desperate to forget
but cannot banish before we vanish
and it spits on our grave;
we regret.

Snap

The scars
bestowed her skin like a map,
the stars
and coda,
begin to untap
the gory story,
glory and fury.
Whore? Me?
Snap.

Ungrateful

Hoping to find the forgotten,
begotten gods and lore,
learned, then burned, the damned
returned to womb of whore,
the tomb—mad monument
of insincerity,
mendicants pick poetic form
for posterity.
Pomposity.

Write Revolution

Revel in raw materials,
ingredients indistinguishable
from the finish. I write
to juggle joviality
and disturb the depressing.

My pencil loves expressing,
delving in the dictionary
a genuine delight.
Words will win
my heart tonight.

Ripple

A well awash with wishes,
brimming with our prayers,
the dreams of disillusioned,
a cross each of us bears,
the silver that we part with,
dancing in the air,
sinks with hope of saving
a soul thought worse for wear.

Night Notes

Three, three, three,
my personal witching hour,
three, three, three,
always the same,
and I say an hour,
but it is only seconds
of sentient thought
(a lucid moment
left uncaught)
that passes with the power
of three, three, three,
rarely recollected,
almost never collected
in the notebook
left by my bed
for the very purpose
of trying to see,
what happens in my head
at three, three, three.

Promise

We have all, at some point in time,
stood beside a grave, willing the resident
to return, prayed to any deity we can think of,
that those at rest—could hear us,
that we could see them one last time,
that we might rid ourselves of the guilt, the shame.
We wish we could know they are at peace,
that they heard the unspoken things,
and had not heard the harsh ones.
Some of us have knelt at a grave,
laid down beside the fallen or even thrown ourselves in,
embracing coffins as though they were love.
We have offered souls and threatened gods,
bargained with demons and spent inheritances
on charlatans that prey on the vulnerable,
like pirates bearing down on a canoe,
for the slim chance of eradicating regret.
And though you will grieve, rage and disbelieve,
please,
please do not waste precious moments by my stone
when I am gone. You belong in the realm of the living,
honour me by staying there in life as long as you can,
making memories like the ones I made for you.
Death is an illusion, I live on.
In the tales you tell of me, the promises I kept,
I live on.
I live on in your smiles, in your triumphs,
in your generous charity and moments of clarity.
I *know* what I meant to you, I *know* how you feel,
And I *know*…
what you are feeling right now will diminish.
I live on.
I promise.

Legacy

If we live on in the memories of others,
I plan to give much to recall,
if we live on in the evidence of success,
I shall record all of your smiles,
if we live on in the dreams of our children,
I will nurture their imaginations,
if we live on in the faith of our gods,
I must worship your beautiful eyes,
if we live on in our literature,
I plan to write a masterpiece,
if we live on in the lives we have touched,
I will endeavour to be legion,
if we live on in the promises we keep,
I intend to be immortal.

Acknowledgements

Thank you to my brother Damien Davis for his stunning cover art.

Thank you to Black Pear Press, and especially, to Polly Stretton, my editor, mentor and nurturing friend.

Thanks, as always, to a loving family, fantastic friends, and kind readers.

A special thank you to Mike Alma and Paul Lenzi, the advice and guidance is treasured, as are you.

About The Poet

Kieran Davis lives in the city of Worcester, with his beautiful wife and wonderful children. Fondly referred to as 'Baldy', he also writes as 'Baldypoems' (Google that and you'll find his popular poetry blog).

Kieran is a keen advocate for writers and writing in all forms, supporting local artists and the Worcestershire Literary Festival whenever possible. He is a proud member of the Worcester Writers' Circle and believes he is the most fortunate man alive, proof that fortune has nothing to do with money, as he is skint.